Seamore at Camp Hosanna
Learning What's Expected

Written by **Carol Craven Bates**

Illustrated by **Kari Wimsatt**

Centerville, Tennessee

For everyone who has ever had a dream, I give you Psalm 37:4:

"Delight thyself also in the Lord and He shall give thee the desires of thine heart."

ISBN: 978-0-9980791-2-7

Copyright © 2021 by Jolly Journey Publishing

Printed in the United States of America

Chapter 1

Week one of camp was over and everyone had gone home except Seamore. The smotter stayed at camp because he didn't have any particular place to be. For him, home was wherever he happened to be at the moment. He woke up early on Saturday morning and headed to the lake for breakfast. When the smotter was somewhat full and refreshed he moseyed back up to the cabin area because he wanted to see if anyone had changed their mind and stayed over for the weekend. The smottosaurus was disappointed when he found every cabin empty and quiet. *"Camp Hosanna is fun when it's full of people but it's a lonely place when you're here all alone. I need to go exploring and see if I can find some new friends. There may be fun and food right around the corner and I don't even know about it."*

Seamore followed a small path through the wooded area behind the cabins. Soon the trail came to a point where he had to make a decision. Directly ahead of him was a large field in which the smotter could see cattle grazing contentedly. The pasture had a fence all the way around it and seemed to take in a very large area. To his right and left was a wide dirt road with trees lining each side that looked as if it may lead to a town full of people. *"This is more like it! Vehicles can travel on this road. This must be the road the children take when they come to camp. Maybe I'll see some of them along the way."*

The smottosaurus chose to turn left. He walked down the dirt road for a couple miles and was disappointed that it never came to an end or back to civilization. *"Boy what a waste of a good road! There isn't anything here but trees. I need to go back toward the camp and explore in the other direction. This road doesn't seem to be going anywhere. It's just boondocks that goes on forever."*

Seamore backtracked for what seemed like hours. When he finally got to the path that led back to Camp Hosanna he stopped to rest and think about what to do next. *"Phew, I'm tired of walking and I'm getting mighty hungry. I think I need to go back to the nice cool lake at camp and wait until evening to check out the other end of this road."*

The smotter spent the remainder of the day just resting in the pond. The most strenuous things he did were swimming, eating and singing. As evening approached, Seamore decided to go exploring again. On this trip he turned right on the wide dirt road. This time the fence and large field were on his left. The herd of cattle he had seen earlier was still quietly nibbling on grass. The

smotter scanned the pasture and in the distance, he could see several small ponds and two very large ones. *"It's strange that I didn't notice all those ponds earlier. I need to go right over there and check them out. Two of them are rather large so they must be full of nice juicy fish. I think that will be a good place for me to have dinner tonight."*

As the smotter cut through the field and around any cows that were in his path he thought, *"The good thing about these ponds is that they're really close to camp so I can come here often and fish. I don't even mind crossing this pasture to get to them. I'm liking Michigan better already."*

Soon after Seamore left for his second stroll, the youth minister for the Word of God Church came by the camp to check on him. Ben searched around the lake, checked inside the cafeteria and even looked in the smotter's cabin, calling out his name several times but to no avail. *"That's strange that Seamore isn't here. I wonder where he could be. I hope he hasn't gone far and remembers to come back. We sure don't want him to cut out on us before the rest of the camping season is over. I guess I'll check on him again tomorrow afternoon."*

The first pond the smottosaurus came to was rather small but he didn't let that stop him from jumping right in. For it to be so small the smotter was surprised that it was very deep and filled with hundreds of baby fish. *"I think I'll let these little guys grow up and get more meat on their bones. They wouldn't be much of a snack at this size. I'll check out one of those larger ponds because the way I see it, larger pond means larger fish."*

Seamore was right. The bigger pond did have much bigger fish. *"Oh wow, look at all these lovely Rainbow Trout! There are some prize winners in here. I'm sure glad I didn't settle for those baby fish. I think I'll just spend the night right here in this pond. There's no need for me to sleep in the lake at camp or in that lonely cabin. As long as I'm back by the time the children start arriving on Monday no one will even know I've been gone."*

Sunday afternoon Ben returned to the campgrounds to see if the smottosaurus had reappeared. To his disappointment there was still no Seamore to be found. *"I better call Mike and encourage him to brush up on the lessons he prepared before we knew if Seamore was going to show up. He may have to fill in as campfire coach after all. If the smotter fails to return by Monday the preacher will have to take over the coaching position."*

Seamore spent Saturday night and all-day Sunday enjoying his newly discovered pond. Just before dusk on Sunday evening he noticed a bright red pickup truck coming across the pasture and heading right to *his* pond. *"Oh goody! It looks like I'm about to have company."*

Mr. McBride pulled his truck up to the edge of the pond and jumped out yelling, "Hey, get out of that pond you wretched otter!" Then he hurried back to his truck to fetch his shotgun. He quickly returned and shot three rounds into the air while he continued to shout.

The smotter had been floating on his back when he first saw the truck coming his way. When he heard all the yelling and then the shots, he realized his company wasn't going to be friendly. He quickly dove deep into the pond and waited for everything to quiet down again.

Jackson McBride sat in his truck for a long time watching the water but the strange looking otter he discovered in his pond didn't resurface. It was starting to get dark and he needed to finish his chores so he poured feed out for the fish and left. When Seamore heard the truck leave he hurried out of the pond, across the pasture, climbed the fence and scurried back to the campgrounds. *"Phew, I thought that guy with the gun would never leave! That fella has an anger management problem. Oh well, I needed to be back on the campgrounds in the morning anyway. I guess I'll sleep in my cabin tonight where it's safe. There sure isn't any need to put myself in danger of an irate neighbor."*

By the time Seamore reached his cabin it was completely dark so he decided to go right to bed. He had just puffed up his pillow and bunched his blanket into a comfy nest when he heard a vehicle pulling into the drive. He was thankful that he hadn't turned on a light so no one would know he was there.

Wondering who would be coming to camp at that hour the smotter peeked out his window. It was too dark for him to see if the vehicle was a car or a pickup truck, specifically a red pickup truck. He heard the engine turn off and saw the headlights go out. Then he watched as someone got out of the vehicle and switched on a flashlight. The smotter tried to look closer to see if the visitor had a shotgun in his other hand but it was way too dark to tell.

The individual holding the light walked down to the lake and Seamore could see the bright beam scanning the area. As he continued to watch he saw the person retrace his steps and come closer to the cabins. That's when he started to get a little nervous. The light and its owner were coming right toward his cabin! *"This is giving me the heebie-jeebies! I think this is a good time for me to skedaddle out of here."* As quickly and quietly as he could, the smottosaurus slipped out the back door and into the woods.

The smotter never knew who the visitor was or when he left. He was in a safe place and that was all that was important. When the sun came up in the morning Seamore was still curled up in a ball under a tree in the forest.

Chapter 2

Ben Richards was the first one to arrive on Monday morning. He was intent on finding out if Seamore had returned to camp. Right behind him was the preacher who was also interested to learn the whereabouts of the smotter. Both men exited their vehicles at the same time.

"Good morning, Mike. It seems like you had the same idea I did. I wanted to get here early and check on our coach."

"Yes, that was my thought too. I need to know if I have to rearrange my schedule and be prepared for tonight's campfire meeting. I don't mind telling you that this uncertainty is starting to wear on my nerves."

"Yeah, I know what you mean. We've never had to deal with anything like this before." Ben flashed Mike a smile as he stated, "I guess excellence comes with a price."

The smottosaurus was swimming in the lake when he noticed that the preacher and youth minister were pulling into the campground. After he finished his snack, he hurried out of the water and across the small wooded area to meet them. They all came together in front of the cafeteria. Seamore greeted them as if nothing was amiss or had changed since they left camp on Friday afternoon. "Hi, Mr. Mike. Hi, Mr. Ben. Are you ready to start another week of camp?"

Mike and Ben looked at each other in disbelief but both felt a sigh of relief flow through their bodies. "Where have you been? I came by to check on you Saturday and Sunday afternoon and you weren't here either time."

"Sorry I missed you, Mr. Ben but I didn't know you were coming. I went exploring and didn't get back until last night."

"That's strange because I was here last night too and you weren't here then either. It was well after dark by the time I finished up at the church and had time to get over here."

"Oh, was that you with the flashlight, Mr. Ben? I was afraid you had a shotgun too."

"What are you talking about? I don't even own a shotgun. I have children coming in and out of my house all the time and I would never have a firearm around them."

Just then Seamore spotted a bright red pickup truck getting ready to turn into the Camp Hosanna driveway. "Uh oh, let's talk about this later. If you'll excuse me, I think I'll take a little dip in the lake." Before either man could respond the smotter took off in a fast trot toward the water.

The two men turned their attention to their visitor. "Good morning, Jack. Step out and join us in the cafeteria and I'll make you a cup of coffee."

"Good morning, gentlemen. Thank you, Mike but I can't stay. I have way too many things to take care of today. As you know I have a cattle ranch to operate and I also raise trout for game fishing competitions. Not only that, but I also have a fish hatchery and sell fish to people who want to stock their own ponds. If I don't keep moving, I can't get everything done."

"I just came by to tell you I found an otter in one of my ponds yesterday. You're not going to believe this but that otter looked as if it had bluish green fur instead of brown although it may have been the glare of the water that made his coat look blue. I know one thing, if I see him again, he's going to have a load of buckshot in his britches. I can't afford to have that thing eat up all my stock."

"I know you have a spring-fed lake over here and that you have it stocked with catfish and tilapia. I just wanted to warn you to be on the lookout because if there's one of those vermin around here there may be a whole family of them. You could lose a lot of fish in a hurry if you let them get out of hand."

Ben cleared his throat before he spoke, "Jack, we have a problem and it goes much deeper than you know. That wasn't a blue otter that you saw it was a blue smottosaurus. Maybe you better take Mike up on that cup of coffee. Please come inside and let us explain."

Soon the three men were seated around a table in the cafeteria with a cup of coffee in their hands. Mike Barlow began with a summary of who Seamore was and why he was in the area. When he finished giving his account, Jackson McBride just sat there quietly and stared at him.

Finally, Mr. McBride responded with, "That's preposterous! That story is so absurd there's no way it can be true. First of all, dinosaurs have been extinct for a long time. If that isn't enough, who ever heard of one that had bluish green fur and could talk? Mike Barlow, you're telling me a tale and I'm not buying it for a second."

Ben gave out a long sigh, "No Jack, it's not a joke. Everything Mike just told you is true. Seamore is here and he's just as Mike described him to you. There's no way we could make up a story that bizarre if we tried. We forgot all about you having a fish farm behind us and about your hatcheries too. It seems like we have forgotten a lot of things when it comes to that smotter."

Mike expressed his concern for any loss of fish their neighbor may have incurred. "Jack we can't tell you how sorry we are that Seamore found his way over to your ponds. We should have known with a smottosaurus in the area there wasn't a safe fish anywhere in the state. If you can figure a value of the stock that was lost, we will surely reimburse you."

"We will also have a chat with our friend Seamore. We know the smotter isn't malicious or defiant, he just doesn't understand that some of the things he does is wrong. As soon as he knows what's expected of him, he is willing to comply."

"Alright, I'll leave it at that. Right now, I can't say how much damage has been done but I'll look closer and get back with you when I know for certain. I appreciate your concern and that you'll make sure it stops. We've been good neighbors for many years and I want our friendship to continue for many more."

The men shook hands and Mr. McBride left to go back to his farm. Just as he was driving out, Preacher Mike observed that some of the counselors and children were starting to arrive for camp. "Ben, you need to be here for the campers right now. I'll go find Seamore and explain our predicament."

When the preacher reached the lake the smotter was nowhere in sight. *"Oh brother. Now where has he gone? I saw him heading this way. I sure hope that smottosaurus hasn't taken a zigzag and gone back to the McBride ponds.*

I have a 10 o'clock appointment and I don't have time to track him down."

Before leaving the campgrounds Mike made a point to inform Ben that he couldn't locate Seamore and that he had to leave for an appointment. "It will be up to you to find time to search for the smotter and make him understand that he can't visit the McBride ponds ever again." Then he added, "I just hope he isn't over there right now."

Chapter 3

Ben realized the magnitude of the problem if Seamore continued to visit the neighbor's ponds and empty them of their fish. The youth minister decided talking to the smotter needed be top priority so he put one of the counselors on his post at the receiving table and left immediately to locate the missing smottosaurus.

Ben first checked around the lake area even though Mike said he had already looked there. Then he thought of the cafeteria but the smotter wasn't there either. Finally, he looked in Seamore's cabin. When that effort came up empty Ben was starting to panic. He decided to check the lake again even though he didn't have much hope. If the smotter wasn't there he would go over to the McBride farm and look around.

At the water's edge Ben called Seamore several times and was surprised when a fuzzy, bluish green head popped up out of the water. "Hi, Mr. Ben. Is your visitor gone? Is it time for the children to start arriving?"

"Yes, to both of your questions, now where have you been? Mr. Barlow and I have been looking all over for you. We need to discuss something very important with you right away."

"I've been right here in this lake for a long time. I didn't know you were looking for me. What is it you want to talk about?"

"You'll have to come out of the water because this matter is far too important to have all this distance between us. I want to see the whites of your eyes and have your undivided attention."

"Okie-dokie, Mr. Ben. This sounds serious. Did your visitor bring his shotgun?"

"Yes, it is serious and no, Mr. McBride didn't bring a shotgun. Is that why you've been hiding out in the lake? Were you frightened by our neighbor shooting his gun in the air yesterday?"

"Yes sir, Mr. Ben. When Seamore hears shootin', Seamore goes scootin'."

"That's a very good policy to have but it would be even better if you avoided provoking someone to that point. Seamore, your visiting our neighbor's ponds and his shooting his shotgun is exactly what I want to talk to you about."

"Listen closely with both of your ears. You cannot go back over to Mr. McBride's ponds and eat his fish ever again. He stocks those ponds and then game fishermen pay him money to fish there."

"You mean people pay to go fishing? That's crazy. Fish are free. God made fish the same day He made me. There were fishes before there were people. The Bible tells us that on the fifth day the Lord said, 'Let the waters bring forth abundantly and let them be fruitful and multiply and fill the waters in the sea.'"[1]

"That's right, God did make fish to fill the sea but we're not talking about the sea. We're talking about Mr. McBride's ponds. Jack has a lot of money invested in his fishing business and if he loses his fish, he'll be out of business."

"Seamore, that's our neighbor's livelihood. You're used to swimming in the ocean where you can eat your fill and that's okay. When you start eating fish that belong to someone else, that's a different matter."

"Wow, this is getting more serious by the minute. You mean I can't eat the fish in this lake either? Mr. Mike told me I wouldn't starve if I came here but now I can't eat the fish and I'm not allowed to be in the kitchen because the ladies are in charge of that. Mr. Ben, I might have to leave camp and go back to the sea."

"Mercy no, please don't leave Seamore! I guess I'm not explaining this right. You may freely eat of all the fish in our lake, just don't venture into our neighbor's ponds. We also have plenty of food in the cafeteria for you if you will just allow the ladies to do the cooking. It certainly is not our intention to make eating a hardship for you while you're at camp. It's a matter of establishing boundaries and coming up with a plan that's beneficial for all involved. Everyone at Camp Hosanna is aware of the fact that you need extra food. If you'll promise not to go fishing in Mr. McBride's ponds, I'll ask the kitchen staff to make sure you have larger portions of food. Do you think that arrangement will work for you?"

"Absolutely, Mr. Ben. As long as I have plenty of chow, I don't care where it comes from. Those trout sure were tasty but I like other food items too."

"Wonderful, I appreciate your willingness to make this work. Let's go greet the children and welcome them as they arrive."

"Okie-dokie, Mr. Ben but first let's go talk to the cooks and see if they'll give me a snack to hold me over until lunchtime."

Chapter 4

Βy midafternoon all the children that were planning on coming to camp for that week had arrived. Seamore and the children were gathered under the shade of the trees between the swimming pool and the lake. "Boys and girls, what do you do if you're on one side of a large body of water and you want to be on the other side?"

Matthew yelled out, "You get in a boat and float across!"

"What if your friends have the boat and they already left without you?"

Several children answered at the same time. "You wait for them to come back and get you." "You swim across." "You walk around the water to the other side."

"Those are all good answers but did you ever try to walk on water?"

Danny shouted, "Nah, nobody can walk on water!"

"That's not completely true. Most people can't walk on water but the Bible tells us of one man that walked on water and another man that took a few steps."

"It happened right after Jesus fed the multitude with the five loaves and two fish from the little boy's lunch. They were beside the Sea of Galilee and Jesus told His disciples to take the boat and go over to the other side. He wanted to stay with the people a little longer and then send them away. Besides that, Jesus wanted to be alone for a while so He could pray."

"I was in the Sea of Galilee that night too. I saw their boat and as far as I could tell it was the only one out there. The water was beginning to get a little choppy and I knew that meant there was a storm coming. I always like to be on hand when there's a storm brewing because it makes fishing a lot easier."

"During the night Jesus decided He wanted to be with His disciples again so He just walked out on the water toward their boat. Sure enough, a storm had developed and the disciples were having a hard time rowing toward where they wanted to go. It was dark but they could still see what looked like someone walking on the water and coming right towards them."

"The disciples were fishermen and they knew people didn't normally walk on water. They thought they were seeing a ghost and they started yelling. I swam a little closer so I could hear what they were saying."

"Jesus heard all the shouting too so He said, 'Don't be afraid guys it's just me.' Peter wasn't sure about that so he said, 'If it really is you, Lord, invite me to come to you on the water.'"

"Jesus answered with one word. He said, 'Come.' Peter hopped out of the boat and started toward Jesus and for a few steps he was doing fine. Then the wind blew really hard, a big wave came by and Peter took his eyes off of Jesus and looked down at the water and was scared again. The minute he let fear grip his heart he started to sink."

"Jesus reached out His hand and pulled Peter back on top of the water. He said, 'Oh you of little faith, why did you doubt?' Then they both got into the boat and just as soon as they stepped inside, the storm ended and the water was calm again."[2]

"I was glad I found that story in the Bible because I knew no one would believe me when I told them I saw someone walking on water unless I had some written evidence to back me up. Actually, I've walked on water a few times myself."

Philip sneered, "Oh yeah, prove it. There's water in the swimming pool and in the lake. Let's see you walk on one of them."

"I can't. It's not cold enough. The water I walked on was frozen. I guess the closest people can come to walking on water is when they're water skiing. The problem is, if the boat stops, they'll be like Peter and sink like a rock."

The whistle blew announcing it was mealtime and everyone scampered toward the cafeteria with the smotter in the lead. He liked being the first in line at chow time and always managed to do just that. It never crossed his mind that he should be polite and let others go first once in a while.

Seamore was pleasantly surprised when Ms. Frances handed him a plate of food that was piled high and running over. He carefully placed it on his tray and proceeded down the line. Ms. Gloria was the next cook that the smottosaurus came in contact with and she gave him another plate of food piled just as high as the first one. Near the end of the food station Ms. Ruby and Ms. Debbie presented the smotter with two more generously filled plates of food. By now Seamore was running out of room on his tray so he just plopped them down on top of the ones that were already there.

As he looked down at his heaping tray of food he said, "I think we *all* did real good. Thank you, kind ladies, for all this grub. That's the best way to show me your love. You know what they say, 'Nothin' says lovin' like extra food on your plate or something like that.'"

Ms. Nellie was at the very end of the serving line and she didn't offer the smotter anything except a glare and a frown. Seamore looked up at her and shivered. He quickly lifted his tray from the rail and trotted off to the first table he came to. As he sat quietly waiting for the others to be served and the prayer to be offered, he thought, *"Mr. Ben must have talked to the ladies in the kitchen about giving me more food. Now I have to keep my promise and not eat anymore of shotgun man's yummy trout."*

Chapter 5

Monday evening Mike Barlow opened the campfire meeting with prayer and words of encouragement for all the campers to have fun and be safe while they were at Camp Hosanna. Ben followed him by leading everyone in songs of praise. Before the youth minister turned the meeting over to Seamore he promised to reward everyone with the biggest banana spit they had ever eaten if they would sit quietly and listen to their coach. Everyone cheered when they heard what their treat for the evening would be. The smotter hurried to the platform to begin the lesson.

"Boys and girls, did you ever wonder how the Israelites got their name? It's kind of a long story because you have to start back with Abraham. When he was seventy-five years old, he and his wife, Sarah, were living in a town called Haran. On today's world map that would be in the country of Turkey. Haran was an important city and a busy place but I never liked it very much. They had some strange religion. They worshipped the moon god not the true God that made the moon. I could never stay there very long because it always gave me the shivers."

"One day God spoke to Abraham and told him to leave his home and start

walking. The Lord said, 'I'll tell you where you're going when you get there.'
Abraham and Sarah packed their belongings and started on their journey. They
traveled a long way and covered a lot of territory. When they got to Canaan the
Lord appeared to Abraham and said, 'This is it. I want you to live right here.' It
was called the land of Canaan back then but it's called Israel now.[3] Since the
land was called Canaan all the people living there were considered Canaanites,
even though there were other "ites" living there like the Hittites, Amorites and
Jebusites."[4]

"The Lord told Abraham, 'I'm going to give you all this land and a big family
too.' Abraham and Sarah had been married for a long time and were getting
kind of old and they still didn't have any kids. When they found out they were
going to have children they got really excited.[5] They waited and waited but years
went by and they still didn't have a child."

"Finally, the Lord told Abraham He was ready to fulfill His promise and give
them a child. By now Abraham and Sarah were really old so it came as a big
surprise for them to learn that Sarah was going to have a son. Abraham was 99
and Sarah was 90 so that meant they were both well past child bearing years.
Their old age didn't stop God because He can do the impossible and just like the
Lord said, in exactly one year they had a bouncing baby boy. They named their
baby Isaac, because that's the name the Lord picked out for him. Isaac means
laughter. The Lord picked that name because Abraham and Sarah both laughed
when they heard they were still going to have a child even though they were so
old."[6]

"Isaac grew up around the Canaanite people but his dad tried to keep him
away from them as much as possible. When his son was old enough to get
married, Abraham started to get worried. He was afraid Isaac would want to
marry one of the women in that area but Abraham didn't want that to happen.
The people of Canaan didn't worship the Lord God Jehovah and Abraham was
afraid they would lead his son away from God. He decided he needed to help

Isaac out and find him a wife. In Bible times that was the common thing to do, to find your child a spouse. Now days everybody does their own picking."

"I was just about to chow into the mutton stew Abraham was serving when I heard him ask Eliezer his oldest and most trusted servant to go back to Haran where the rest of his family lived and fetch a wife for Isaac among his people. Eliezer was willing to go but he was nervous because he was afraid the lady he picked wouldn't be willing to move to Canaan. After Abraham convinced him it would be okay if she refused to relocate, he loaded up ten camels with gifts and supplies and headed out."[7]

"I'm glad I decided to go with them on the trip. It was a long way but the camel ride made it fun. I'm also glad they took plenty of food along with all those gifts. After all, when you're hungry you can't eat bracelets and earrings."

"When we got back, Abraham told us that Isaac had been anxiously waiting for his bride to arrive. His dad said every day he would look in the direction the caravan would be coming until one day it finally came into sight. He was excited because he wanted to settle down and start his own family."

"After the couple got married, I left there and went back to the sea. When I came back a long time later, I was surprised to see that Isaac and Rebekah still didn't have any children. One night I heard Isaac praying for his wife. The Lord answered that prayer by giving them twins. The Bible tells us that those babies were scrappers and were wrestling even before they were born. It got so bad, Rebekah prayed and asked God why it was happening. The Lord said, 'There are two different nations inside you. One will be stronger than the other and the oldest will serve the youngest.' When they were born Esau was born first so that made him the oldest and means he would serve his brother. Normally in their culture all his younger siblings would be subordinate to him but God had other plans. Jacob was born just a few seconds later and as he was being born, he reached out his hand and grabbed Esau by the heel. This is where the story gets exciting."

"The twins were different in every way including the way they looked. Esau had red hair and was very hairy. He liked to be out in the forest and hunt and for some reason that made his dad love him best. Jacob had smooth skin, liked to cook and hang around home so that made his mom love him more. Being the firstborn would normally entitle Esau to the birthright. That means he would receive a double portion when it came time for him to inherit his father's wealth but remember, God had told Rebekah that wasn't going to happen this time."

"Over the years I stopped by to check on them from time to time and I think Rebekah must have told Jacob what God said about the oldest serving the

24

youngest because he decided he wanted the birthright and he came up with a plan to take it away from his brother."

"One day Jacob was making some wonderful smelling stew. I asked him what he called that stuff and he said it was pottage. I told him to be sure and put plenty of meat in it because I like my stew really meaty. Later when Esau came in from hunting, he was starving so he asked Jacob for some of that stew. Jacob declared, 'Okay you can have some of it but you have to give me your birthright.' Esau snapped back, 'Sure, it won't do me any good if I die of hunger. You can have the birthright, now give me some stew.' Jacob was thinking of the future and Esau was only thinking of the here and now."[8]

"Hey, you know what? I'm thinking of the here and now too. All this talk about stew is making me hungry. We don't have time to finish the story tonight so let's eat those yummy banana splits Mr. Ben was talking about and we'll finish the story tomorrow."

Chapter 6

When Seamore woke up the next morning, he was surprised to see that several of the boys were already outside so he hurried to get out there with them. "What are you looking at fellas?"

"Someone left two big baskets full of tomatoes in front of the cafeteria door. What do you think they plan to do with these?"

"I don't know guys but they sure do make good hand grenades when you're playing war, even more so when they're really ripe like these are. Do you want to go to battle?"

That's all the encouragement they needed because the boys grabbed a tomato in each hand and started pelting Seamore with them. "Hey, no fair! I'm outnumbered. Let's divide into two units. That way we can each have a basket of ammo."

The skirmish took place right in front of the cafeteria and in just a matter of seconds tomatoes were coming from every direction. Soon tomato parts were plopping down all around like globs of red snow.

The loud shouts and giggles brought a couple of the counselors out of their cabins in short order. Ben was the first one on the scene, "Whoa! Stop that! What are you doing wasting all those tomatoes? I'm sure we can put them to a much better use than this."

That's when it happened. A tomato struck the youth minister right on the forehead. Seeds and juice ran down his nose and dripped off his chin but Ben just stood there in stunned silence. When Seamore realized what had happened he yelled, "Hold your fire troops! We have a casualty. Our Commander-in-Chief has been wounded."

"Sorry, Mr. Ben. We didn't know you were going to be in the line of fire. You shouldn't sneak up on us like that."

"I didn't sneak up on you! I came out yelling. You should all know better than this, especially you Seamore. Whose lamebrain idea was this anyway?"

All hands pointed to the smotter but it was Hunter who spoke for the group. "Seamore said tomatoes make good grenades and asked if we wanted to have a war but we threw the first bomb so I guess we're all guilty."

"Yes, I agree you are all guilty and you shall all be punished. We'll discuss this after breakfast but right now I want everyone to go get cleaned up and be back here by the time the ladies have breakfast ready. Now scat before I lose my cool."

By this time the rest of the campers and counselors were gathering around the area. Ben asked the counselors to take the children back to their cabins until they heard the breakfast whistle and then when they came to eat, they should enter and leave by the back door.

After everyone was assembled in the cafeteria and the prayer had been offered, Ben announced that everyone involved in the tomato fight were to remain in their seats after eating because he wanted to have a talk with them. All the others were free to enjoy the swimming pool or to visit the craft tables.

Forty minutes later, Ben, Seamore and twelve boys were the only ones left sitting at the tables in the dining room. The five cooks were in the kitchen cleaning up but everyone else had left the building.

Ben stood before the group and stated, "Well I found out where all those tomatoes came from. Mr. J.B. Lakelon, one of our camp board members, had them delivered because he thought the campers would enjoy having BLT sandwiches for lunch today. Because of your unthoughtful behavior that won't be happening. Here's what will be happening instead. I've gathered everything you'll need to clean up that mess. You're to go out there and make it look like it never happened. I want the front of the building washed down along with the door and the windows. Shovel or sweep away whatever is on the ground. You can put it in buckets and dump it in the garbage can behind the building. When you're through with all that I want each of you to come back in here where you'll find pencils and paper on the table. I want you to write a letter of apology to Mr. Lakelon. This is all to be completed before lunch is served at 12 o'clock. You may now be excused to get started."

The cleanup went fairly quickly but the letter writing was more of a challenge. Seamore labored the most because he couldn't get his thoughts down on paper.

Dear Mr. J.B.,
"Thank you for all those nice, juicy tomatoes. I'm sure they would have been very tasty in a BLT sandwich but they made wonderful grenades too."
Your friend,
Seamore

When the smotter finished his letter, he slipped it into the pile with the others and hurried outside to find his friends. After everyone had gone, Ben read each letter and when he got to Seamore's he just shook his head. He quickly jotted a note of his own before he put all the letters in a large envelope and had someone deliver them to Mr. Lakelon's home.

Chapter 7

By Tuesday evening Seamore had forgotten all about the tomato incident that occurred earlier in the day. He was completely focused on finishing the story he started the night before.

"Boys and girls, last night I was telling you how the Israelites got their name. We got down to the part where Esau sold his birthright to his brother, Jacob, for a bowl of stew. Nothing changed in their household situation for a long time. Then when Isaac was much older and thought he was about to die he told Esau to go hunting and bring back some venison. That's deer meat. He told his son, 'You make me something savory to eat and I'll give you the blessing of the firstborn.' When I heard him say make something savory to eat it made me listen a little a closer. I decided not to stray too far from camp until after dinner."

"It appeared that Isaac wasn't going to pay any attention to the deal the two boys had made. I'm not sure he even heard about it. The sad part is he wasn't going to pay any attention to what the Lord wanted either. Before the boys were born, God had told Rebekah that the oldest would serve the youngest and surely she told him what the Lord said."

"Rebekah must have heard what Isaac told Esau too and thought she needed to help God out because her husband was about to mess up and give the wrong boy the blessing. She hurried to inform Jacob of what was happening. She said, 'Your dad is about to give your brother the blessing. Quick, help me fix some food. You need to go in and pretend to be Esau and get the blessing for yourself.' Now Jacob knew his dad was blind and wouldn't be able to tell who was standing before him but he was afraid Isaac might reach out and touch him and feel how smooth his skin was. He mumbled, 'Esau is hairy and my father will know I'm not his firstborn.' Rebekah sighed, 'Don't worry about that. I'll wrap goat skins around your hands and put some on the back of your neck too. You can even put on some of your brother's clothes that smell like the forest and your dad will never know it's not Esau he's talking to.'"

"Isaac was blind but he wasn't a dummy. He questioned how his son got back with a deer so soon and wondered why the voice he was hearing sounded like Jacob instead of Esau. He reached out and felt his son's hands and smelled his clothes. Finally, he was satisfied he was speaking to his firstborn and that's when he gave Jacob the blessing instead of Esau. God had promised the birthright to Jacob so actually he was trying to steal something that was already his."9

"Jacob managed to deceive Isaac but now he was in a lot of trouble with his brother. When Esau came back from hunting and found out how Jacob had stolen his birthright, he was furious and wanted to do his brother bodily harm. Rebekah could see that things were about to get ugly so now she had to come up with a plan to get Jacob away from there for a little while. He needed to stay away until Esau had time to calm down. Isaac and Rebekah were both in the wrong. Rebekah for encouraging Jacob to lie to his father and Isaac for not asking the Lord how to handle the problem about the birthright. The Lord would have worked out the situation if Isaac had prayed and Rebekah had waited for God's timing. That would have avoided any feuding in the family but now they were in a big ole mess."

"All of a sudden Rebekah had to go into damage control mode to protect Jacob from his brother. She knew Isaac didn't want their son to marry a Canaanite woman so she asked him to send Jacob back to Haran, where she grew up, so he could look for a wife. I guess she figured she could kill two birds with one whack or something like that. Her plan worked and soon Jacob was on his way to Haran."

"I thought I'd go along with Jacob to keep him company and to see how he would choose his wife. Along the way Jacob had to stop and sleep because it was getting dark. He didn't have anything to put his head on so he piled up some stones and used them for a pillow. During the night he had a dream that he saw a ladder reaching from earth to heaven with angels going up and down on it and he saw the Lord standing above the ladder. The Lord introduced Himself and promised to bless Jacob and his descendants and bring him back home someday. That's when he woke up and was afraid because he realized God was in that place and he didn't even know it."

"Jacob was wide awake by then so he got up and made a pillar out of his pillow. In other words, he piled up the rocks he was sleeping on and made an altar. Then he poured oil over it and made a vow to the Lord. He said, 'If God will be with me and bring me back home in peace, the Lord will be my God.'"[10]

"Jacob had a long walk ahead of him and he had a lot of time to think of all the things he'd done wrong. He was probably missing his family by now. I bet he was wishing he was back home where he could whip up some more of that tasty stew he knew how to make. I know that's what I was thinking about."

"When Jacob got to Haran he did find a wife. He fell in love with his Uncle Laban's daughter, Rachel. He agreed to work for his uncle for free for seven years just to get to marry her. When it came time for the wedding his uncle deceived Jacob by giving him his oldest daughter Leah to marry instead. Later he got to marry Rachel too but he had to agree to work for his uncle

for another seven years. The deceiver found out what it was like to be deceived. Jacob found out the hard way that you always reap what you sow."[11]

"Now days it's illegal for a man to have more than one wife but during that period of time it was accepted. As the years went by, Jacob ended up with four wives and twelve sons. The sad part is that he picked up a bad trait from his parents. He treated some of his family members like they were more valuable to him than the others. His favorite wife was Rachel and his favorite son was Joseph. This behavior would cause trouble for him in the future just like it did for his mom and dad."

"There was also a lot of hostility between him and his uncle so one day Jacob decided to take his family and move back to Canaan. It had been many years since he left home but the closer he got to it the more he began to worry. He was afraid Esau might still be mad at him for stealing the birthright when he was younger so Jacob decided to send some of his servants on ahead with gifts for his brother. When they came back and told him Esau was coming towards them with four hundred men he really got scared."[12]

"Jacob couldn't stand the stress anymore so he decided he needed to get off by himself so he could pray and think. When he was finally alone, the Angel of the Lord appeared before him in the form of a man and they started wrestling. Jacob didn't know he was actually wrestling with God at first but sometime during the night he realized it. They wrestled all night long and in the morning the Angel of the Lord wanted to get away so He touched Jacob's thigh and made it come out of joint. Jacob cried out to God, 'I'm not going to let you go until you bless me.' The Lord said, 'Tell me your name.' When Jacob told Him, the Lord said, 'I'll change it to Israel.' After that the descendants of Jacob were called the children of Israel. The name Jacob means supplanter or to replace. It was God's plan for Jacob to replace his brother Esau. Now the Lord was giving him a new name. Israel means Contender with God or 'a man who wrestles with

God'. They were called Hebrews sometimes too but that's because of the language they spoke."[13]

"So, boys and girls, the answer to the question of how the Israelites got their name is, Abraham's grandson Jacob had his name changed to Israel by God. Whenever you hear the name Israel, you'll know that they are the descendants of Jacob. The land where his family lived is now called the country of Israel."

The smotter put his nose in the air and started sniffing. "You know what? I think I smell fresh baked apple pie and that smell is coming from the building where we have our chow. Let's go see if my nose knows what it's talking about." The children all fell in line behind Seamore and they all hurried to the cafeteria.

Chapter 8

Wednesday morning as soon as breakfast was over, Seamore and the children gathered in their favorite spot, in the shade of the trees in front of the swimming pool. "Boys and girls, last night I told you how Jacob had his name changed to Israel by the Lord while he was in the process of moving his huge family and all his flocks back to Canaan. Sometime after they got settled into their new home his son Joseph had a couple of dreams and those dreams got him in a lot of trouble."

Hunter laughed as he shouted, "That's crazy! A dream can't get you in trouble because you're asleep in your bed when you have a dream."

"You're exactly right. The dreams didn't get him in trouble until he got out of his bed and went and told his family what his dreams were about."

"Joseph had eleven brothers and ten of them were older than he was. The older ones didn't like Joseph very much because he was their daddy's favorite child and they were jealous of him. Mommies and daddies aren't supposed to love one of their children more than the others but Jacob surely did and he didn't try to keep it a secret."

"Jacob gave Joseph gifts that he didn't give to his other sons. One thing his daddy gave him was a special coat of many colors. That made his brothers furious so they started saying mean things to Joseph."

Emma proudly announced, "My mommy and daddy love me and my sister the same. They never buy just one of us new stuff."

"I'm glad you have parents that love you both. That's the way it's supposed to be. Good parents never favor one child over another but some children aren't that fortunate."

"One night when Joseph was a teenager, he had his first dream and in the morning he told his brothers about it. He said, 'We were all in the field binding sheaves and my sheaf stood up straight and all your sheaves gathered around and bowed down to my sheaf.'"

"I know you're wondering what a sheaf is so let me tell you. A sheaf is bundles of grain that the reapers have cut and tied together. It's gathered up and tied with a string to keep it from falling apart, kind of like a farmer does when he has a bale of hay. Sometimes those sheaves were left in the field for the poor people to take."[14]

"When Joseph told his older brothers about his dream that made them hate him even more. He was insinuating that they were going to bow down to him and they knew that wasn't going to happen. He was just a kid and they wanted him to respect them."

"Later on, Joseph had a second dream. That time he dreamed that the sun, moon and eleven stars all bowed down to him. He told that dream to his father along with his brothers and of course that made Jacob upset with him too. His daddy said, 'Do you think your mother and I and your eleven brothers are actually going to come and bow down before you?' That wasn't their custom and Jacob was offended by the very idea."

"One day sometime after his second dream while I was sitting in the shade and munching on some lamp chops, I heard Jacob ask Joseph to go to Shechem to check on his older brothers. They had to take their father's flock a long way off to get enough food for all the sheep. They had been gone a long time so Jacob was starting to get worried about them."

"Joseph went to the place where his father sent him but his brothers weren't there. He had to ask a man in the area if he had seen them and the man told him they had to move their flock to a better food source. He instructed Joseph where to look and finally he found them."

"The brothers saw Joseph coming from a long way off and their jealousy surfaced again. It's never a good thing when you allow jealousy to control your thinking because it will cause you to do or say things that you will regret later on. Just because a bad thought comes to your mind you don't have to keep thinking of it, you can choose to think of something good instead.[15] The Lord wants us to fill our hearts and minds with love. In fact, He commanded us to love everyone even our enemies.[16] When you're jealous of someone you can build up a hatred toward that person. Some of Joseph's brothers were in a dangerous place. Their jealousy had turned to hate and now they were thinking of how to get rid of him permanently."

"One of them came up with an idea. He said, 'Here comes the dreamer. Let's kill him and throw his body in a pit. We can tell dad a wild beast ate him and then we'll see what becomes of his dreams.'"

"His oldest brother, Reuben, heard what his brothers were planning to do to Joseph and he wanted to put a stop to it. He protested, 'No, don't take his life. Let's just toss him into a pit.' Reuben was thinking later on when his brothers weren't watching he would rescue Joseph out of the pit and take him back home."

"When Joseph arrived at their camp his brothers stripped off his pretty coat of many colors and threw him in a pit nearby then they sat down to eat a meal. As they were eating, they saw a caravan of Ishmaelites traveling from Gilead to Egypt. The Ishmaelites had a bunch of camels that were loaded down with spices and they were coming very close to their camp. That's when Judah came up with a brilliant idea of how to get rid of Joseph. He smugly declared, 'What profit is it if we kill our brother and cover up our deed? Let's sell him to the Ishmaelites. After all, he is our own flesh and blood so we shouldn't kill him.'"

"Ruben wasn't there at the time but the rest of them agreed it was a good idea so they went ahead and sold Joseph for twenty pieces of silver. One of the camels knelt down and I hopped on so I could tag along. I heard Joseph yelling at his brothers. He was begging them not to do that wicked deed but they just laughed and said again, 'Now we'll see what becomes of your dreams.'"

"Later on, Reuben came back to get Joseph out of the pit and he was shocked to see that he wasn't in there. He was so upset that he tore his clothes in horror. He was afraid of his father's anger because being the oldest son, Reuben knew his dad would hold him responsible for letting anything happen to their little brother."

"Now they had to come up with a lie and another plan to cover up what they had done. They decided they would kill a goat and dip Joseph's coat of many colors in the blood. They would tell their daddy they found it and make him believe a wild animal had killed Joseph. Their plan worked very well because Jacob believed their lie and he was very sad. His family tried to cheer him up but he refused to be comforted. It broke Jacob's heart that his favorite son was no longer with him. He didn't know that Joseph was still alive and on his way to Egypt."[17]

I felt really bad for Jacob not knowing his son was alive and well. I wanted to go back to his house and tell him what happened but I learned a long time ago to stay out of the affairs of humans. I found out that sometimes the Lord allows people to go through hard times so they will learn the lesson He wants to teach them. Besides that, I didn't want those ten mean brothers after *me*.

"Boys and girls, this is the second time Jacob was being deceived. The first time was when his Uncle Laban switched brides on him and he married Leah instead of Rachel, so Jacob was still reaping what he sowed. Always do the right thing and you won't have to reap something bad later on."

"Hey, did you hear that noise? It came from my tummy. It's telling me it's hungry and I need to send down some food. Whenever I hear that noise, I know it's time for a snack. Let's go see if the ladies have it ready yet. We can finish this story later."

Chapter 9

After their snack, Seamore and the children played games until it was lunchtime and then the afternoon was spent in the cool water of the swimming pool. Suppertime was especially enjoyable because Mr. Lakelon had sent over enough fresh corn and watermelon so everyone could have corn on the cob with their meal and ice-cold watermelon for dessert.

That evening at the campfire meeting, Seamore was anxious to continue the story about Joseph. The smotter planned to tell the children how God turned Joseph's trouble into triumph.

"Boys and girls, remember how I told you Joseph's ten older brothers sold him to the Midianites because they were jealous of him? They didn't like the fact that their dad loved him more than he loved them. They also didn't think much of the dreams their little brother had."

"The Midianite caravan was on its way to Egypt where they were going to sell their wares and sell Joseph as a slave. As soon as we got there, I hopped off the camel I was hitching a ride on and changed into Egyptian clothes. I wanted to keep a low profile. I didn't want anyone to get the idea of selling me as a slave too. I stayed out of sight because you know what they say, 'Out of sight out of sale or something like that.' A man named Potiphar bought Joseph. He was the captain of the guard, which means he was the man in charge of all the soldiers guarding King Pharaoh."

"Mr. Potiphar took his new slave to his house where Joseph worked hard and did everything his master wanted him to do and God blessed Joseph and made him prosper. When Potiphar saw that God was with Joseph and he noticed how he was getting richer because of having him around, he put Joseph in charge of everything he had. The Bible tells us that Potiphar didn't worry about anything he had at home except for the food he ate."

"Everything was rolling along good until one day Potiphar's wife accused Joseph of doing something he didn't do. Mr. Potiphar didn't know the truth so he believed his wife and locked Joseph up in the king's prison."

"The Lord knew Joseph was innocent so God blessed him while he was in jail too. The chief jailer soon realized God was with Joseph so he put him in charge of all the other prisoners. In fact, he was in charge of the whole prison."

"One night there was a big blowup at the palace and the king got really mad at his chief cupbearer and his chief baker. The king was so furious with them he had them both put in prison."

"Everyone in the kitchen was worried that they might be next. It scared me too so I found a good hiding place next to the pantry and tried to lay low for a while. Pharaoh had the power to lob off your head if he wanted to and I wanted to keep all my body parts intact."

"After those two had been in jail for a while they each had a dream on the same night. The next morning Joseph could see that they were sad and he asked them what was wrong. They told him they had a dream but they didn't know what it meant. Joseph informed them, 'God can interpret dreams. Tell me what your dream was about.'"

"The cupbearer announced, 'I saw a vine that had three branches on it. It budded, bloomed and produced ripe grapes and I squeezed out the juice and gave it to Pharaoh.'"

"Joseph declared, 'The three branches represent three days. Within three days the king will restore you to your office and you will be his chief cupbearer again.'"

"Then Joseph added, 'Keep me in mind when things go well with you. Tell Pharaoh to get me out of this jail. I was kidnapped from the land of the Hebrews and besides that, since I've been here, I haven't done anything worthy of being put in prison.'"

"When the baker heard the favorable interpretation that the cupbearer received, he said, 'I also had a dream and in my dream I saw three baskets of bread on my head. In the top basket there were all sorts of baked goods for Pharaoh. The birds came and were eating out of the basket while it was still on my head.'"

"Joseph answered, 'The three baskets represent three days. Within three days the king will hang you on a tree.'"

"Three days later it was Pharaoh's birthday and he had a big party. He restored his cupbearer and he executed the baker just as Joseph had interpreted. The chief cupbearer was happy to be back at work but sadly he forgot all about Joseph and his request."[18]

"Two full years later the king also had a dream. In fact, Pharaoh had two dreams in the same night. He dreamed he was standing at the river and seven fat cows and seven skinny cows came up out of the water then the skinny cows ate the fat cows. The king fell back to sleep and he had a second dream. This time he saw seven good ears of corn on one stalk and then seven skinny ears of corn sprung up and ate all the good ones. I dream about food a lot too but I do it in the daytime. I always sleep at night. Although I do go for a snack if I wake up."

"The next morning Pharaoh called for all his wise men but none of them could tell the king the meaning of his dreams. That's when the chief cupbearer remembered the time he was in jail and how Joseph had told him and the chief baker the meanings of their dreams. He also remembered that they both came true."

"The king was delighted to find out about Joseph being able to interpret dreams and sent for him right away. Joseph was quick to tell Pharaoh it wasn't him that knew the interpretation of dreams, it was God who told him what the dreams meant."

"Joseph told the king that the two dreams were actually the same dream. God was showing Pharaoh what He was about to do. Joseph said, 'The dreams mean that there will be seven years of plenty of food and then seven years of famine.' Then Joseph added, 'The famine will be so severe that the years of plenty will be forgotten. The fact that the dream was repeated shows that it will come to pass in the near future.'"

"Joseph stressed that Pharaoh needed to appoint someone wise to oversee collecting all the extra food during the seven good years so it would last through the seven years of drought and famine. The king thought about that for a few minutes then he declared, 'Since God has shown you what is going to happen, I've decided to appoint you as overseer of the food project. Only in the throne will I have more power than you.' Three cheers for Pharaoh. Personally, I think that was the smartest thing he ever did. Joseph was definitely the man for the job. With God blessing everything he did, the food project was bound to be a success. I'm sure glad they had all that food stashed away when pickin's got

slim. I'm also glad I became friends with Joseph during our trip to Egypt. I had no idea he would be in charge of passing out all that food someday. It just goes to show, be good to everyone you meet because you never know who might be the one who gives you food later on down the road."

"Pharaoh made Joseph ruler over all the land of Egypt. He gave Joseph his ring, some royal clothes to wear and a gold chain. Joseph was also given a chariot so he could ride right behind Pharaoh and everyone had to bow down to him."

"Pharaoh told Joseph that no man could lift a hand or foot in all the land of Egypt unless they went to Joseph first. That means everyone in Egypt or from any other country would have to deal with Joseph to do any business. The king wanted Joseph to feel at home in Egypt so he gave him an Egyptian name and a wife so he could have a family."[19]

"The seven years of abundance seemed to fly by but the seven lean years were kind of draggy. It was very disturbing to see all that food dry up. It makes me hungry just thinking about it."

"Folks, we won't have time to finish this story tonight either and besides I don't think I can go on without a snack. Whenever I start talking about food it isn't long before I can't stop thinking about eating. That's the point I'm at right now."

The smotter didn't wait for anyone to agree or protest. He simply left the platform and headed to the lake in a fast trot. The youth minister jumped off his seat by the campfire and shouted. "No, Seamore come back! We're going to go have cookies and milk right away." Seamore stopped in is tracks and turned around. He said, "Okie-dokie, Mr. Ben but let me grab a couple of fishes first."

Chapter 10

Thursday morning right after breakfast, Ben surprised everyone by announcing they were all going for a boat ride. The counselors divided the children up into small groups and gave them each a boat trip around the lake. Seamore was thrilled to be able to play in the water and have the children nearby. He would dive down and bring up turtles, frogs and big fish to show them what was under the water.

He was also glad to have time to have a few extra snacks along the way. It seemed like mere minutes until the children were all back on shore and ready for their snack. The smottosaurus was surprised the morning had passed so quickly. *"Wow! I can't believe it's snack time already.*

Most days it seems like forever until chow time again." Of course, he had forgotten about all the fish he had eaten while he was in the lake.

As soon as the food was gone, the smotter asked, "What do you want to do until it's chow time again?

One of the girls shouted out, "Let's play hide and seek!"

"Okay, that's a good idea but first let me tell you about the very first time I ever heard of hide and seek."

"It happened a long, long time ago but it wasn't a game back then. It was real life. It wasn't done the same as it is now either. Back then, everybody hid and God did the seeking. Of course, there were only two people here at that time."

"It took place in the Garden of Eden. There were lots of fruit trees there and the Lord told Adam and Eve they could eat from any tree they wanted to except one certain tree. That tree was called 'The Tree of the Knowledge of Good and Evil.' The Lord warned them that if they ate from that tree, they would surely die.[20] That tree was there as a test to see if the people would love God enough to obey Him. I'm sad to say that they failed the test."

"As soon as they ate some of its fruit, their eyes were opened and they knew they had sinned and failed God and they were afraid. Later when the Lord came to the garden, they hid among the trees and He had to find them.[21]"

"You may have wondered why your mom and dad take you to church every week, send you to camp in the summer and tell you stories from the Bible. Well, let me tell you the reason."

"At the exact time Adam and Eve ate the forbidden fruit is when sin entered the world. At that moment mankind died spiritually and from that point every person needed a savior. That's why everyone must accept Jesus as their savior and be baptized so they will be forgiven of their sins and be alive spiritually again.[22] Before you leave camp this week you may want to consider doing that. If not this week, keep it in mind for the near future. Our hide and seek is just a game but the first time it was done, it wasn't.

When Seamore finished the story, he said, "Okay boys and girls, do you want to go play our game now?"

Everyone just sat there quietly for a few seconds until Hunter jumped up and yelled, "Yeah, and you're 'it'! We'll hide first and you come find us." With that statement made, the children all bolted out of the cafeteria and scattered like ants coming out of an anthill. By the time most of the children had taken a turn of being 'it', the noon whistle blew, announcing it was lunchtime, to which Seamore was very thankful.

Right after lunch the smotter gathered the children together in their shady spot. He was anxious to get to the next part of the story of Joseph. "Boys and girls, remember how King Pharaoh made Joseph in charge of all the food and made him ruler of Egypt? Now instead of being a slave or in prison, Joseph was in a place of prominence and just like in his dreams everyone was going to have to bow down to him."

"Joseph had been gone from home for a long time. He was only seventeen when his brothers sold him into slavery and he was in Egypt for thirteen years after that. That means Joseph was thirty years old when Pharaoh promoted him to be ruler of Egypt. His dreams were finally becoming a reality but it had been a long time. Much longer than the dreams of the chief cupbearer or the king."

Steven wanted to know why. "How come Joseph had to go to jail and wait a long, long time for his dreams to come true but the other guys only had to wait a little while?"

"That's a very good question but the Bible doesn't tell us why. All I can tell you is that it wasn't God's time for it to happen. Maybe the Lord was preparing Joseph's heart or it could be that He was preparing Pharaoh or the older brothers' hearts. One thing is for sure, when God wanted it to happen, it happened."

"During the seven years of plenty, Joseph gathered up all the extra food and stored it away for later on. When the drought and famine finally got there, it wasn't only in Egypt, it was worldwide. Joseph's family back in Canaan were hit by the famine too. When Jacob heard there was grain and food in Egypt, he sent his sons, all but his youngest son, Benjamin, to get some of it. He didn't want his youngest son to go for fear he would lose him like he did Joseph."

"When the brothers arrived in Egypt, they had to go to Joseph to ask for food and they had to bow down before him when they did the asking. Joseph recognized them and remembered the dreams he had when he was a teenager. His brothers didn't know it was Joseph because he was dressed in Egyptian clothes and they thought he was just another guy from Egypt."

"Joseph wanted to know about his dad and his little brother so he asked a lot of questions about their family. They told him their father was still alive, that they were all brothers and that they had a little brother named Benjamin still at home. Joseph thought he'd have some fun with those guys. He told them he didn't believe them and accused them of being spies. To show he meant business, Joseph had all ten of them put in prison for three days. I guess he wanted them to get a taste of what he went through all those years."

"When Joseph let his brothers out of jail, he told them the only way he would believe they weren't spies is if they brought their little brother to Egypt. Just to make sure they would come back, he was going to put their brother, Simeon, in jail again and said he would stay there until they returned with Benjamin."

"Even though none of the brothers recognized Joseph they started to feel this trouble they were having was a result of what they had done to their little brother years ago. They freely discussed that possibility in front of Joseph. He had been speaking to them through an interpreter so they didn't know he could understand every word they were saying. What they said touched him and made him cry but he didn't let his brothers see his tears. He wasn't ready to tell them who he was just yet. Instead of showing tenderness, Joseph had Simeon hauled off to jail right before their eyes."[23]

"When the brothers went to Egypt, they took enough money to pay for the food they needed but Joseph had left instructions that their money was to be put back in their sacks before they left. The men didn't know it was there and didn't find out about it until they were on their way home. When they discovered it, they were scared to death because they knew they would be accused of stealing from the Egyptians and were afraid the Lord was using this to punish them for what they did to Joseph. I think it's funny how the Lord kept bringing that thought to their mind. After all those years they were still feeling guilty for what they had done."

"As soon as the men arrived home, they told their father everything that happened and how the man of Egypt had spoken roughly to them. They had to tell their daddy that they couldn't go back to Egypt for more food unless they took their little brother with them. Jacob was very upset when he heard that news.

Chloe had a question and her hand shot up at the same time she asked, "Why was Jacob so upset? Joseph wouldn't hurt his little brother and if he saw Benjamin, he would let Simeon out of jail and give them more food."

"That's a great question. Jacob didn't know what we know. All he knew was that he had lost Joseph, Simeon was in jail in Egypt and he may lose Benjamin too if he let him out of his sight. Jacob had no way of knowing that the man in Egypt was really his son Joseph."

"At first Jacob said Benjamin definitely could not go to Egypt but finally the famine got so bad he agreed to let him go. The brothers were to take gifts for the man in Egypt along with double the money to buy more food and to pay for the food they had gotten the first time."

"At that time Egypt was the only place on land where there was an abundance of food so if I wasn't swimming in the sea, I was in Egypt. I was thankful that I had just gotten back to Egypt and into my Egyptian clothes when the brothers arrived. You should have seen Joseph. He was thrilled when he saw that his brothers were back to buy more food and that they had brought Benjamin with them. He gave orders to release Simeon from prison and have them all taken to his house so they could have lunch with him."

"The men were afraid when they were taken to Joseph's house. They thought they were in trouble because of the money they found in their sacks from the first trip. They quickly told the house steward that they had brought double the money so they could pay for both trips."

"When Joseph came home for lunch, his brothers gave him the money they brought and bowed down to him again. Remember, Joseph was dressed like an Egyptian official and they hadn't seen him in years so they still didn't recognize him. Besides, they never dreamed their little brother would be in such a powerful position in Egypt."

"Joseph was so glad to see his little brother, Benjamin, that it made him cry so he had to hurry and leave the room. When he finally got control of his emotions, he ordered everyone to sit down to eat. The older brothers were amazed that Joseph had them all lined up at the table according to their age. They couldn't figure out how he knew all their ages to do such a thing. Then when the food was served, Benjamin was given five times more food than any of the others."

"Oh my, all this talk about five times more food is making me hungry. Maybe I better go get a snack to hold me over until the ladies have our next meal ready." Just then the whistle blew announcing that supper time had finally arrived. "Oh boy! Once again, I've been saved by that lovely sound that tells us it's time to get our victuals. Come on! Let's go eat now and we can continue this story at the campfire tonight." Everyone scattered in the direction of the cafeteria and as usual, Seamore was at the head of the pack. The counselors had learned to just stand back when the whistle blew and wait for the dust to settle.

Chapter 11

As Seamore and the children entered the cafeteria they noticed there wasn't any food on the buffet line. The smotter sniffed the air and determined there wasn't anything cooking in the back to bring out to fill those empty wells on the food bar. "That's strange. I distinctly remember hearing the dinner whistle. I wonder what they did with all the chow."

The youth minister asked everyone to take a seat. "Folks we have a surprise for you this evening. We called you in a little early so you would have time to get cleaned up before supper. We usually take care of that after we eat but we'll be eating around the campfire tonight. We can roast hot dogs and marshmallows and make lots of s'mores."

As soon as Ben made the announcement cheers went up all around the room. "Don't take too much time but freshen up a little bit while we start the fire. When you're ready, everyone gather over by the meeting area and we'll pass out long sticks and the hot dogs. Then when everyone is full, we'll be ready for our campfire devotions."

The evening meal was a delightful treat. The children and staff were all enjoying the food and outdoor fun. After everyone was finished eating, Seamore polished off all the hot dogs, buns, graham crackers, marshmallows and chocolate that were left over. He told the ladies he was saving them several trips of taking everything back to the kitchen. The children were getting quiet, they were full and ready to settle down and listen to another lesson. They no longer had to be reminded to sit quietly during the time the Bible story was being presented. They were anxious to hear the conclusion of Joseph being reunited with his brothers in Egypt.

Seamore was excited as he stepped onto the platform and headed for the microphone. "I love this part of the story! Joseph had some hard times in the past but now everything was fixin' to work out really well. Earlier we learned that he had just met his youngest brother that he hadn't seen for thirteen years and now all of them were having lunch together."

"After their time of refreshing, the brothers had to prepare to leave Egypt and go back home. Before they left, Joseph gave them all the food they asked for and a couple of things they didn't know about. He secretly gave them back all the money they brought and had his silver cup put in Benjamin's sack."

"The brothers left Egypt feeling their trip had been a big success. They had the food their families would need and no one had been left behind so their father should be very proud of them. They didn't know it yet but their trip to Egypt was about to hit a snag."

"As soon as they were out of town Joseph sent his steward to go after them. He told his servant to charge them of stealing his silver cup. The brothers were really upset when they were accused of stealing from the ruler of Egypt. They vowed, 'We promise you we didn't take anything. We even brought extra money because somehow last time our money was put back in our sacks.' They were so sure that they were all innocent one of them shouted, 'With whomever the cup is found let that person die and the rest of us will be your ruler's slaves!' Joseph's steward changed the agreement so that only the one that was guilty of stealing would become the slave."

"The search started with the oldest brother's sack and went down to the youngest. Of course, the silver cup was found in Benjamin's sack. The older brothers were so upset and afraid that Benjamin might not get to go home with them that they ripped their clothes to show their distress. In great fear everyone turned around and went back to Joseph's house to try to get it straightened out. When they got there, they again bowed down before him. One of the brothers named Judah, pleaded with Joseph to let him stay as a slave and let Benjamin go home to his father."

"We know how that silver cup managed to be in their sack but at the time the brothers didn't know how it had happened. Judah knew he hadn't taken the cup but he wasn't really sure about Benjamin so he was covering for him. Judah also knew he didn't want to go home without his little brother. He'd rather stay in Egypt as a slave than to face his father without Benjamin."[24]

"Joseph might have been testing them to see if they would leave their youngest brother in Egypt like they sold him as a slave thirteen years before. Joseph got the answer he wanted when he stated that he would keep Benjamin as his slave and they were all free to leave. Judah again spoke up and offered himself in Benjamin's place. That declaration touched Joseph so much that he started to cry. At that moment he realized his brothers had changed over the years."

"Joseph ordered all the Egyptians to leave the room. Then he tearfully told his brothers who he was. He told them not to be afraid of what they had done to him when he was a teenager. He said, 'God sent me to Egypt before you to preserve life. There has already been two years of drought and famine and there are still five more years of it to come.' Then he urged his brothers to go back to the land of Canaan, get their father and bring him to Egypt so they wouldn't starve."

"The whole time his boys were in Egypt, Jacob was worried sick about them. He feared something bad would happen to them and that he might lose another son or two. This time when the brothers got back home, they were all together and they had good news to share. When they told their father that his favorite son was still alive and was the governor of Egypt, he almost had a heart attack. He certainly didn't believe what they were saying."

"The older brothers had a lot of explaining to do and had to confess that they were responsible for Joseph being in Egypt in the first place. After they told Jacob all that Joseph said, showed him the gifts he sent and explained how it happened that he was still alive, their father started to revive. He also started to believe what they were saying."

"It wasn't long before the clan was packed up and on their way to Egypt. Jacob had seventy-one family members that left Canaan. When they arrived in Egypt, they grew to seventy-five because they were now reunited with Joseph, his wife and their two sons. What started out as a sad story turned into a happy life for Joseph and his kin.[25] So you see boys and girls, sometimes when we think there is no hope for things in our life to change and get better, God may be working on something that will turn everything into good just like He did for Joseph. Never stop praying or give up hope."

The smotter hesitated for a just a second before he declared, "I believe its snack time again. I realize we've already had hot dogs and s'mores but that's all gone. My tummy is telling me it's empty. Let's head over to the chow building and see if the ladies have prepared another snack for us. Besides, you guys will be going home in the morning so we need to eat and visit one more time tonight."

In the morning Seamore was on hand to tell all the children, counselors, cooks, and youth minister goodbye. Then he headed to the lake to wait for everyone to pack up and be on their way. Ben was the last one to leave. He decided to go down to the lake and have a talk with the smotter before he left. "Seamore, what are you going to do this weekend?"

"I don't know but I'll have to think of something because it gets mighty lonely with no one here."

"Well, you need to promise me you won't go visit Mr. McBride's ponds while you're here alone."

"Oh no, I won't eat any more of Mr. Jack's delicious trout. When Seamore makes a promise, he keeps his promise. I won't swim in his ponds either because I don't want to be tempted. The Bible says to abstain from all appearance of evil."[26]

"That's right, it does. The ponds aren't evil but if they cause you to be

tempted to do something you shouldn't, you need to stay away from them. Why don't you read a book this weekend? That will keep you busy for a while. I have several I can loan you if you're interested."

"I like to read books but lately I've been thinking about writing one. This might be a good opportunity for me to get started on it."

"Hey, that's an excellent idea. How about if I go to the office and get you a notebook and a pencil. Will that be enough to keep you busy for a couple of days?"

"Sure, that'll be great. Can you find a piece of clothes line for me too? I want to dry some things."

"Of course, that won't be a problem. You must be going to do some laundry. I'll be back in just a few minutes. Is there anything else you want me to bring?"

"Not unless you have a lot of extra food you don't know what to do with. I'll take that off your hands and put it to good use."

Ben didn't even answer. He just smiled and walked away. As he was heading for the office he thought, *"That smottosaurus is an eating machine. I wonder what it would take to actually fill him up."*

About the Author

Carol Craven Bates resides in middle Tennessee but is originally from New Jersey. She enjoys reading, writing and sewing. Carol and her husband have two daughters, two sons and eight grandchildren (one of whom illustrated this book). Through her stories, Carol hopes to encourage boys and girls to learn to enjoy reading. She chose Christian fiction so children would see how exciting the Bible is and how it fits into their everyday lives.

*If you have enjoyed book three of Seamore and his adventures, be watching for book four, "Seamore Loves Camp Hosanna".

[1] Genesis 1:20-23
[2] Matthew 14:22-32
[3] Genesis 11:29-32 & Genesis 12:1-7
[4] Nehemiah 9:7,8
[5] Genesis 13:14-16
[6] Genesis 17:15-17 & Genesis 18:1-15
[7] Genesis 24:1-10
[8] Genesis 25:29-34
[9] Genesis 27:1-29
[10] Genesis 27:30-46 & Genesis 28:1-21
[11] Genesis 29:1-28 & Galatians 6:7
[12] Genesis 30:25-43, Genesis 31:1-18, Genesis 32:3-7
[13] Genesis 32:24-28
[14] Leviticus 19:9&10 & Deuteronomy 24:19
[15] Philippians 4:8
[16] Matthew 5:44 & John 15:17
[17] Genesis 37:1-35
[18] Genesis 37:36, Genesis 39:1-23, Genesis 40:1-23
[19] Genesis 41:1-45
[20] Genesis 2:7-17
[21] Genesis 3:1-9
[22] Mark 16:16
[23] Genesis 41:46-57 & Genesis 42:1-24
[24] Genesis 42:25-38, Genesis 43:1-34, Genesis 44:1-34
[25] Genesis 45:1-28 & Genesis 46:1-27
[26] 1 Thessalonians 5:22

CPSIA information can be obtained
at www.ICGtesting.com
Printed in the USA
BVHW020534180521
607541BV00008B/155